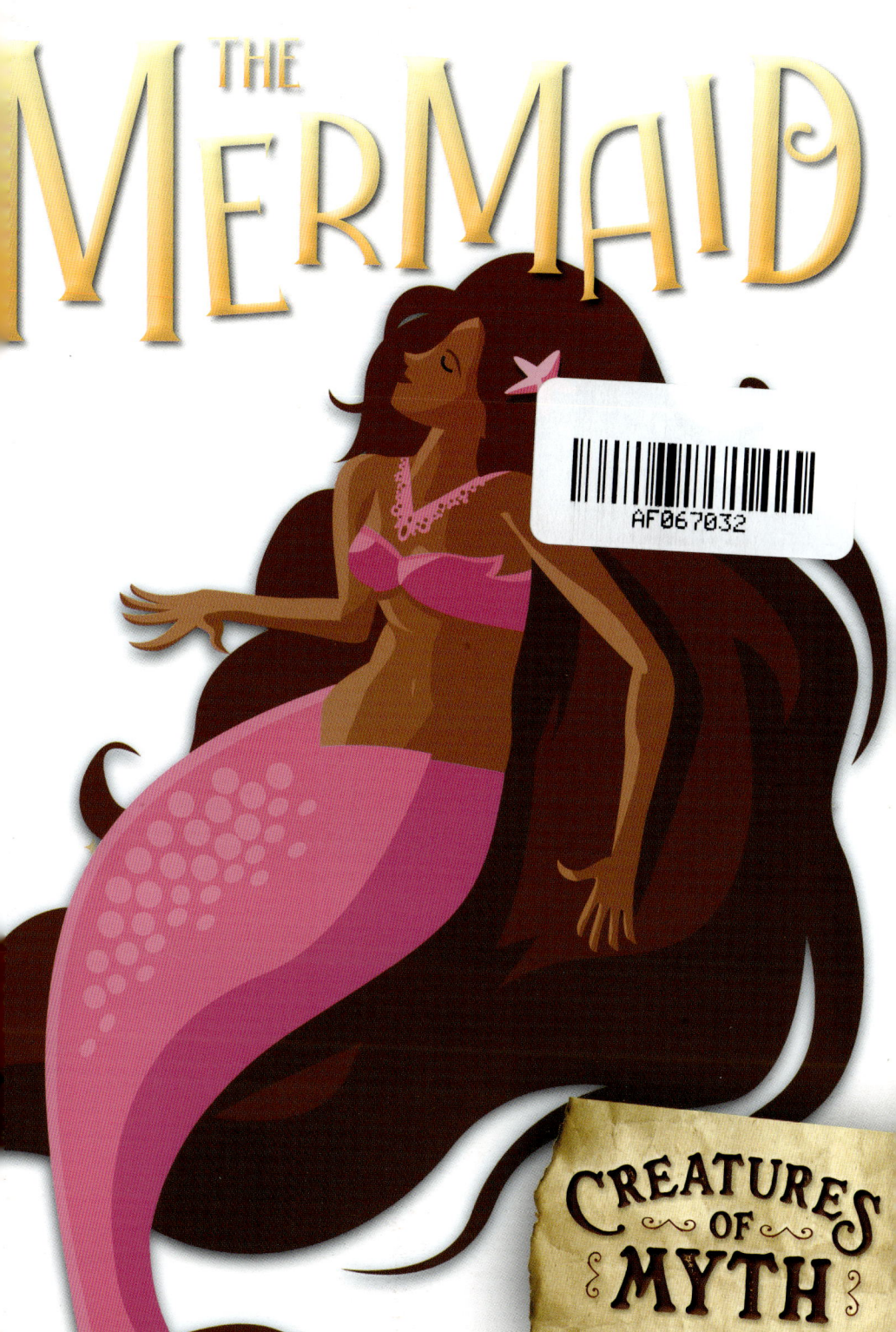

BookLife PUBLISHING

©2023
BookLife Publishing Ltd.
King's Lynn, Norfolk
PE30 4LS, UK

All rights reserved.
Printed in China.

A catalogue record for this book is available from the British Library.

ISBN: 978-1-80505-023-0

Written by:
Charis Mather
Adapted by:
Noah Leatherland
Edited by:
Rod Barkman
Designed by:
Isabella Croker

All facts, statistics, web addresses and URLs in this book were verified as valid and accurate at time of writing. No responsibility for any changes to external websites or references can be accepted by either the author or publisher.

AN INTRODUCTION TO BOOKLIFE RAPID READERS...

Packed full of gripping topics and twisted tales, BookLife Rapid Readers are perfect for older children looking to propel their reading up to top speed. With three levels based on our planet's fastest animals, children will be able to find the perfect point from which to accelerate their reading journey. From the spooky to the silly, these roaring reads will turn every child at every reading level into a prolific page-turner!

CHEETAH
The fastest animals on land, cheetahs will be taking their first strides as they race to top speed.

MARLIN
The fastest animals under water, marlins will be blasting through their journey.

FALCON
The fastest animals in the air, falcons will be flying at top speed as they tear through the skies.

Photo Credits – Images are courtesy of Shutterstock.com. With thanks to Getty Images, Thinkstock Photo and iStockphoto. Recurring images – delcarmat, Zodar, briddy, Gluiki. Cover – delcarmat, Bonezboyz, Irina Markova, Zodar. 4–5 – Toporkova, Toporkova. 6–7 – Gekko Gallery. 8–9 – Maridav, Richard Wonka, Bondarevska Iryna. 10–11 – Damsea, Roman Samborskyi. 12–13 – Andrey_Kuzmin, o_obolenskaya. 14–15 – Pete Niesen, Gekko Gallery. 16–17 – TreesTons, Zwiebackesser. 18–19 – Andrea Izzotti, Firn, Preto Perola. 20–21 – Rich Carey, zcw, vkilikov. 22–23 – scubadesign, Denis Lyapin. 24–25 – EpicStockMedia, Dolores M. Harvey, Kiyoweap (Wiki Commons). 26–27 – Lillac, D2 Photography. 28–29 – Fer Gregory, Stockbym. 30 – SaltedLife.

CONTENTS

PAGE 4 The Mystery of the Mermaid
PAGE 6 Mermaid Spotter's Guide
PAGE 8 A Tale of Tails
PAGE 10 The Power of Song
PAGE 14 Everything We Know
PAGE 16 Do Mermen Exist?
PAGE 18 Easy Mistake to Make...
PAGE 22 Impostor!
PAGE 26 Hidden Hideouts
PAGE 28 The Lost City of Atlantis
PAGE 30 Creatures of Myth
PAGE 31 Glossary
PAGE 32 Index

Words that look like this are explained in the glossary on page 31.

THE MYSTERY OF THE MERMAID

Have you ever seen a mermaid splashing in the water? Probably not. Mermaids are mythical creatures. Mythical creatures are mysterious beings that appear in stories and <u>myths</u>.

No one knows if they are even real. There are lots of stories about these half-woman, half-fish beings. They are famous creatures, so how come we do not see them swimming around?

Some tales of mermaids come from thousands of years ago. Sailors returning from sea have told people about these strange beings and their powers. Stories of mermaids are found all over the world. Could the sailors have been telling the truth?

Imagine a mermaid was found in real life. Would they be like the stories, or would they be completely different?

MERMAID SPOTTER'S GUIDE

If you want to spot a mermaid in the wild, you need to know what they look like:

The top half of a mermaid looks exactly like a normal person. Their bottom half is what to look for. If you see a person with a large fish tail instead of legs, you will know you have found a mermaid!

LARGE FIN
A wide fin helps mermaids swim. This is sometimes called a fluke.

FISH TAIL
Mermaids have <u>scaly</u> tails like a fish.

The myths about mermaids say they all have different tails. A mermaid's tail could be all sorts of colours. They might have some extra fins, too.

LONG HAIR
Mermaids are often drawn with long hair.

HUMAN UPPER BODY

A TALE OF TAILS

Since mermaids have fish-like tails, you might think they could only be found in the sea. However, some stories say that mermaids can <u>transform</u> their tails into legs. All they have to do is dry themselves out and they will be able to walk on land.

There could be mermaids walking among us that we don't even know about!

A mermaid will dry out and become human if they accidentally fall asleep on a rock. Luckily, there is a fix. All a mermaid has to do to transform their legs back into a tail is get wet.

A mermaid taking a trip on land would have to be careful. Just a few raindrops could end up spilling their secret!

THE POWER
OF SONG

As well as being able to transform, mermaids have other magical powers.

Mermaids are wonderful singers. Their songs are more than just beautiful, though... They can also do magical things. If you hear a mermaid sing, you might become <u>enchanted</u>. You may find yourself unable to stop listening.

Mermaids are able to communicate with both animals and humans. This means they can make friends, wherever they are.

Some stories say that animals trust mermaids. There are lots of different creatures in the ocean, including some that can be very dangerous. Mermaids can make them all calm and friendly.

Mermaids are said to be able to control water and the weather. Something upsetting a mermaid might cause a storm to suddenly appear over the ocean.

Making a thunderstorm would be a good way to keep people away from the mermaids' homes. Maybe that is why so many stories about mermaids talk about ships getting wrecked!

Some stories say that mermaids are very lucky. Sailors used to <u>carve</u> mermaids into the front of their ships. They thought it would make the sea calm and easy to sail on.

However, other people think mermaids bring bad luck. Some of the first ever maps had mermaids drawn in places where there was a lot of bad weather and shipwrecks.

EVERYTHING
WE KNOW

Mermaids live much longer lives than humans. It is said that they might live for hundreds or even thousands of years. Maybe all the healthy food they eat helps them to live for so long!

Mermaids like to eat sea plants and seaweed. There is lots of other seafood around them too, such as clams and shrimp.

Mermaids spend hours of their days searching for shells, pearls and colourful pieces of coral.

Mermaids make all kinds of things out of these treasures. They make things they can wear or use, such as combs, jewellery and even musical instruments. If you find a beautiful seashell washed up on the beach, it might be a gift from a mermaid!

DO MERMEN EXIST?

Some people believe that there must be mermen swimming in the seas as well. Together with mermaids, these half-fish, half-human mythical creatures are called merfolk.

There are lots of stories about mermaids but not as many tales about mermen. It seems that mermen are much harder to find. Is there some reason why mermen never seem to come to the surface?

Greek myths talked about a merman named Triton. The Greeks believed he was the son of the sea god Poseidon.

POSEIDON

Triton is often shown with a fork-shaped trident and a twisted shell. The myths say that the shell can be blown like a trumpet and used to control the oceans. The Greek myths said that Triton lives in a golden palace deep under the water.

EASY MISTAKE
TO MAKE...

There are a few creatures in the world that have some things in common with mermaids. You would think it would be obvious if you were looking at a mermaid or not. Lots of people have been tricked by other animals for hundreds of years.

These <u>impostor</u> animals have managed to fool even the world's most famous <u>explorers</u>!

Manatees

Manatees are large creatures that have a wide, flat tails and a pair of flippers on their upper body. Manatees need to breathe air even though they live in the water.

Manatees are famous for being mistaken for mermaids. Sailors have seen manatees coming up to breathe and thought they were mermaids.

Dugongs

Dugongs are similar to manatees and have also been mistaken for mermaids. They have differently shaped tails to manatees. Dugongs have tails that look more like a mermaid's.

Up close, manatees and dugongs do not look like mermaids at all. Those sailors must have been seeing things after being at sea for so long!

Monkfish

Monkfish look strange, but they have made people think they have seen mermaids in the water. Their pink tongues and flat faces have confused sailors in the past.

Again, the water can make things look very different. There are stories of people thinking they have seen human faces in the water, though they have turned out to be monkfish.

IMPOSTOR!
Sirens

Sirens are part-woman, part-bird creatures from Greek myths. They do not look much like mermaids, but they have similar powers. Be careful, though. Knowing the difference between a mermaid and a siren might just save your life!

Mermaids are kind creatures, but sirens are thought to be much nastier towards humans.

Sirens also have magical songs that enchant listeners, just like mermaids. A siren's song is much more dangerous, though. People enchanted by sirens try to get closer to them and end up crashing their boats. Hearing a siren's song is certain doom!

SELKIES

Selkies are half-woman and half-sea-creature like mermaids, but there is one big difference between the two.

When selkies are in the sea, they look exactly like seals. When they get on land, they transform to look like humans. They do this by taking off their seal coat, revealing a woman underneath. If they lose their seal coat, they will not be able to change back.

Ningyo

Ningyo are very similar to mermaids. They are both a mix of fish and human. Ningyo are thought to be much scarier and uglier creatures, though.

Most ningyo are said to have large, fish-like bodies with human faces. They do not sing like mermaids and sirens, but stories about ningyo say they can cause bad things to happen to anyone trying to harm them.

HIDDEN HIDEOUTS

If you are brave enough to go looking for mermaids, the sea is the best place to start. Luckily, you might not need to go very far into the water to find one.

Mermaids are said to like relaxing on rocks by the coast. If you bring them a shiny shell, you may end up making a new friend.

If you are not able to find a mermaid near a beach, the next place to look would be deep under the sea. So much of the oceans have not been explored by humans yet. Who knows what could be hiding under the water?

Be careful if you go looking for mermaids. They are not the only things swimming in the deep...

THE LOST CITY OF ATLANTIS

People have been telling stories about the city of Atlantis for thousands of years. The stories say that Atlantis sat on an island and was the greatest city in the world.

The legend says that the island was hit by earthquakes and floods. After that, Atlantis sank to the bottom of the ocean in one day.

No one knows where Atlantis used to be, or what part of the ocean floor it sank to. Some people think it never existed at all.

An underwater city would be a perfect place for merfolk to make their home. Perhaps mermaids are so hard to find because they live in a lost city?

CREATURES OF MYTH

Mermaids are mysterious creatures. No one knows too much about what they get up to under the sea, but it is always fun to wonder about.

There are lots of stories of mermaids out there. If you want to learn more about these mythical creatures, keep reading about them. Maybe you will be the person who finally finds one!

GLOSSARY

CARVE	to cut a design into a hard material
CORAL	a hard material formed on the bottom of the sea by small animals
ENCHANTED	caught in a spell by something pleasing
EXPLORERS	people who travel to places where no one has been before
GOD	a being that is believed to be more powerful than humans
IMPOSTOR	something that pretends to be something else
MYTHS	stories from the past that may have a mix of truth and made-up things
PEARLS	hard, shiny balls that can sometimes be found in shells and can be used as jewellery
SCALY	covered in small, overlapping flakes that protect the skin
TRANSFORM	to change into something else

INDEX

ATLANTIS 28–29

DUGONGS 20

MANATEES 19

MONKFISH 21

NINGYO 25

SAILORS 5, 13, 19–20

SELKIES 24

SHIPS 12–13

SIRENS 22–23, 25

SONGS 10, 23

TAILS 6–9, 19–20